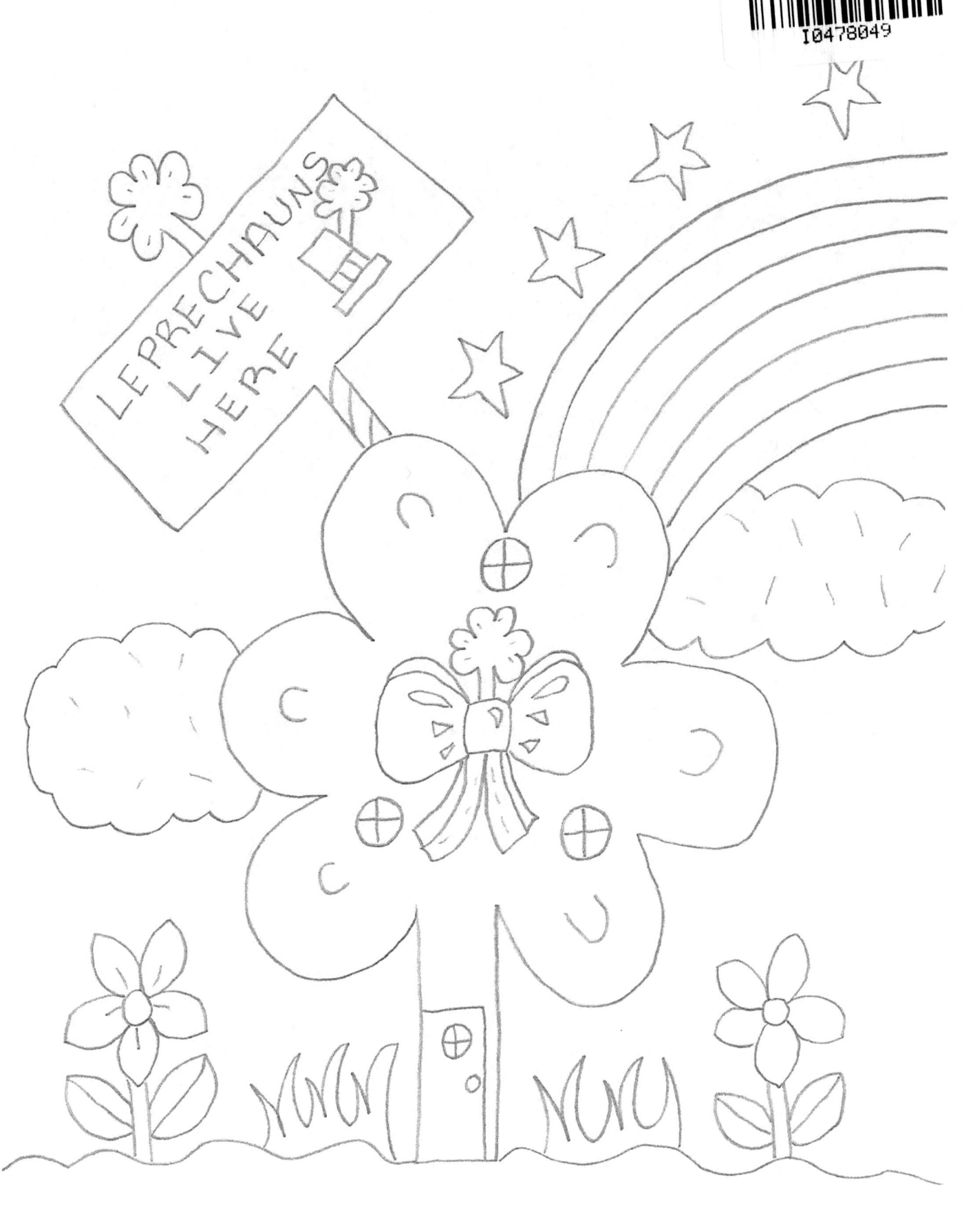

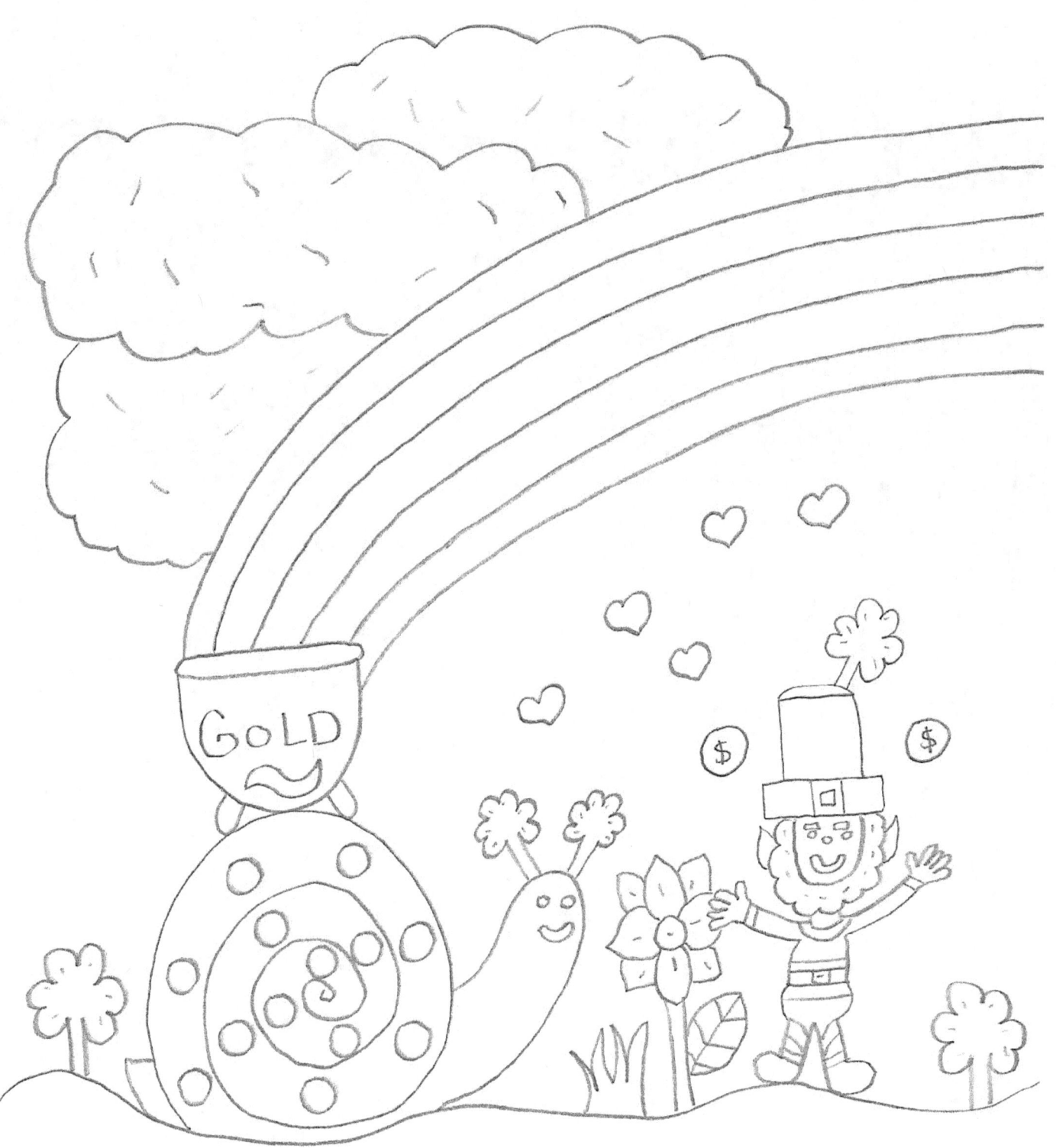

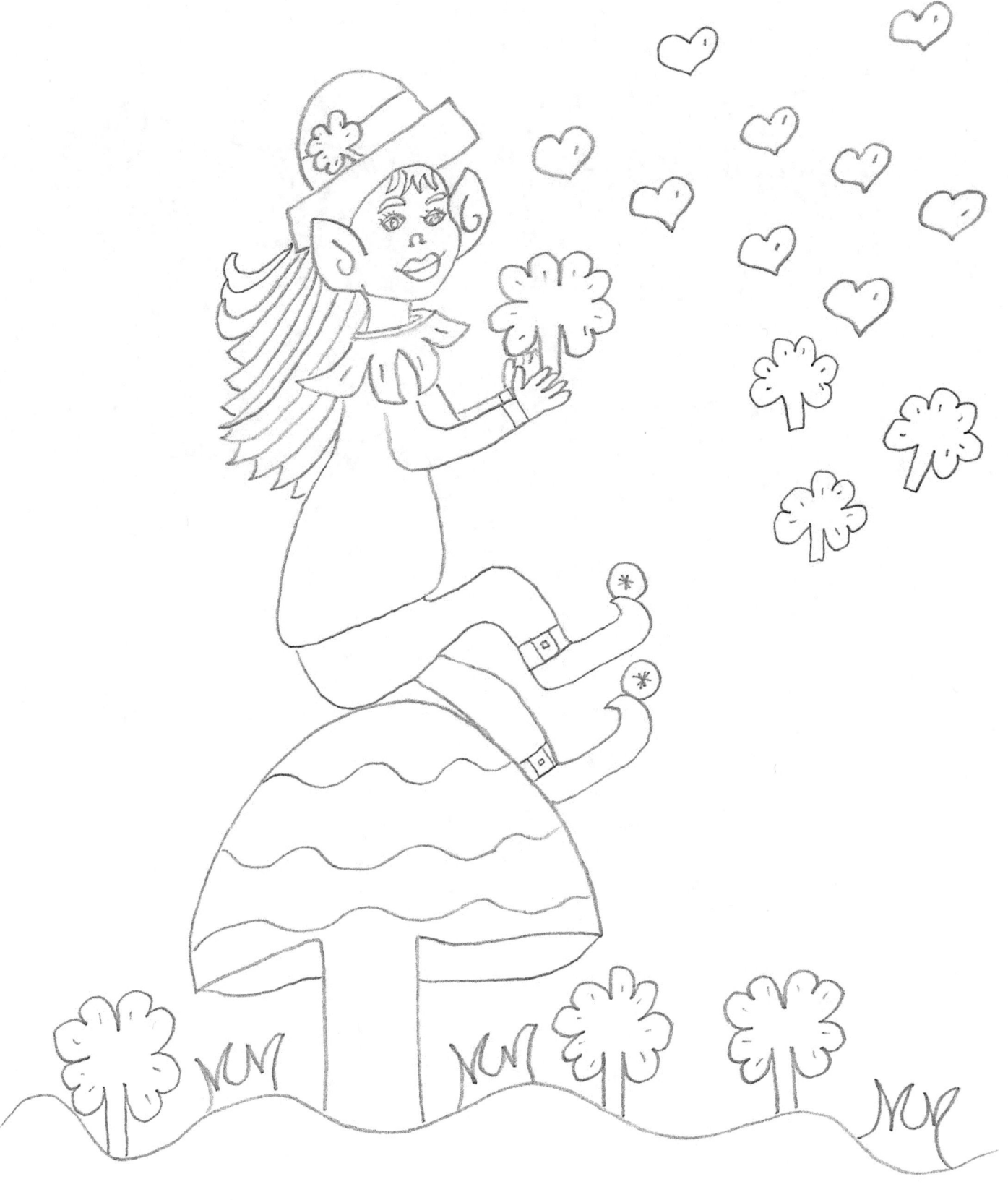

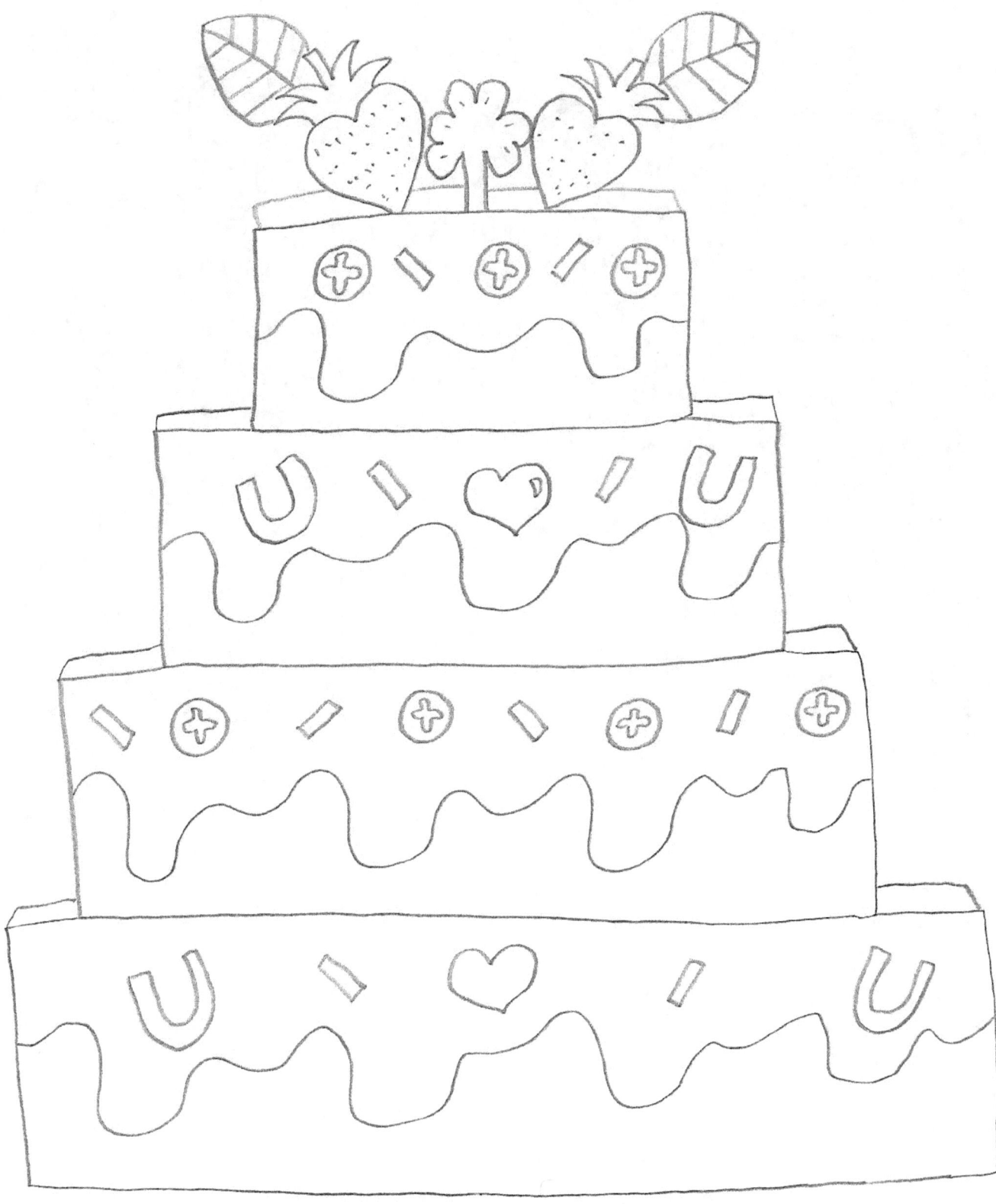

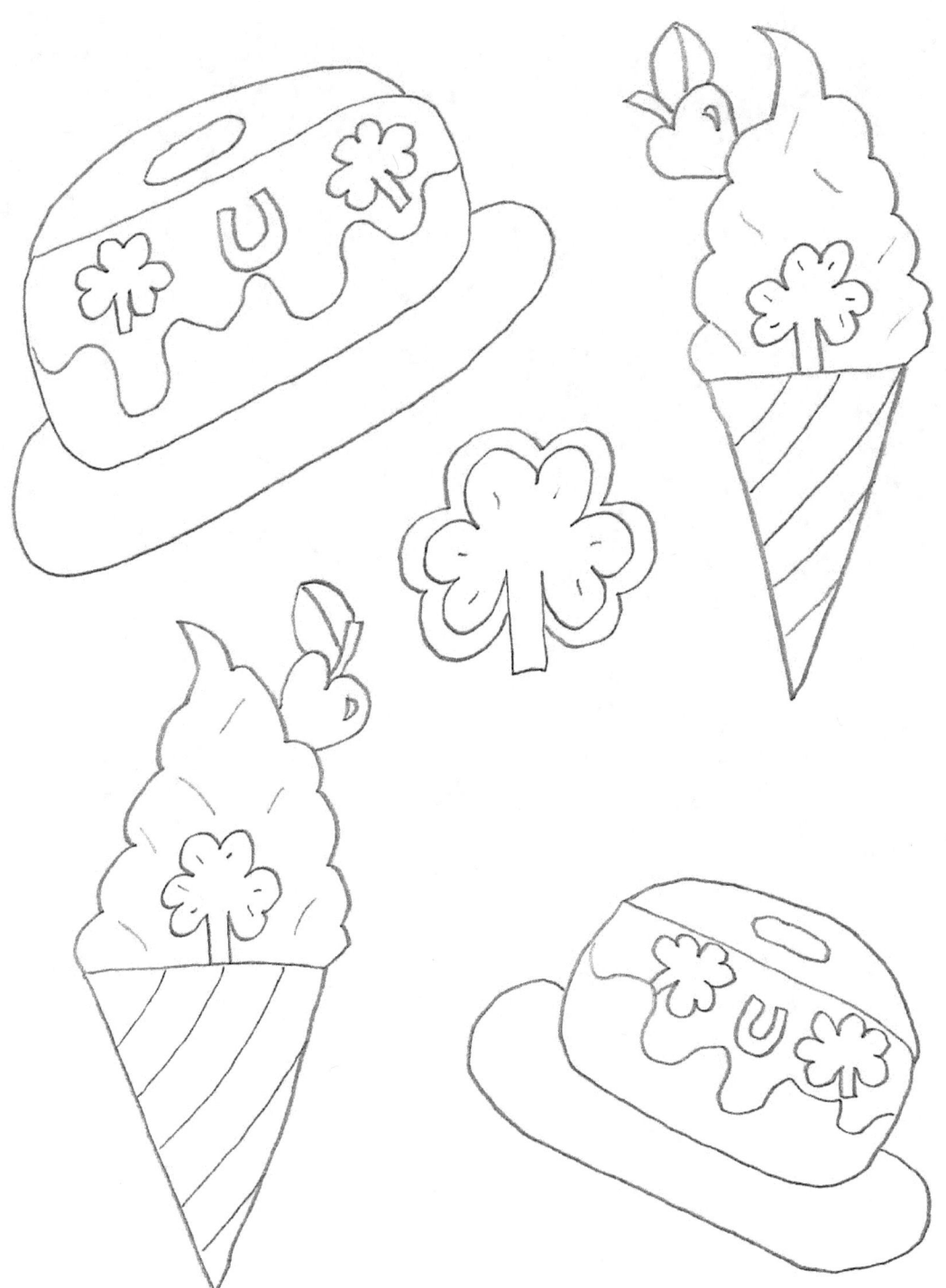

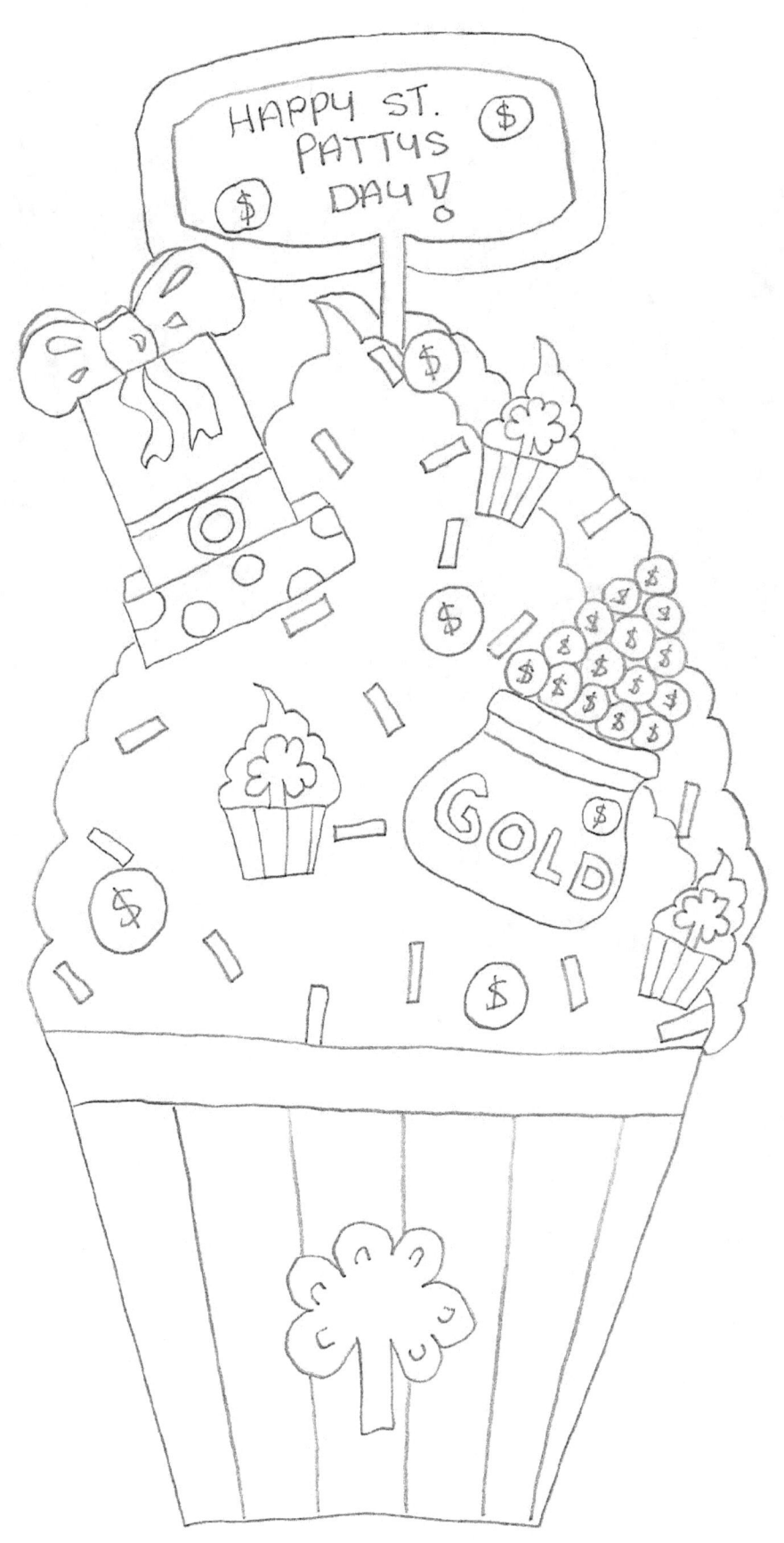

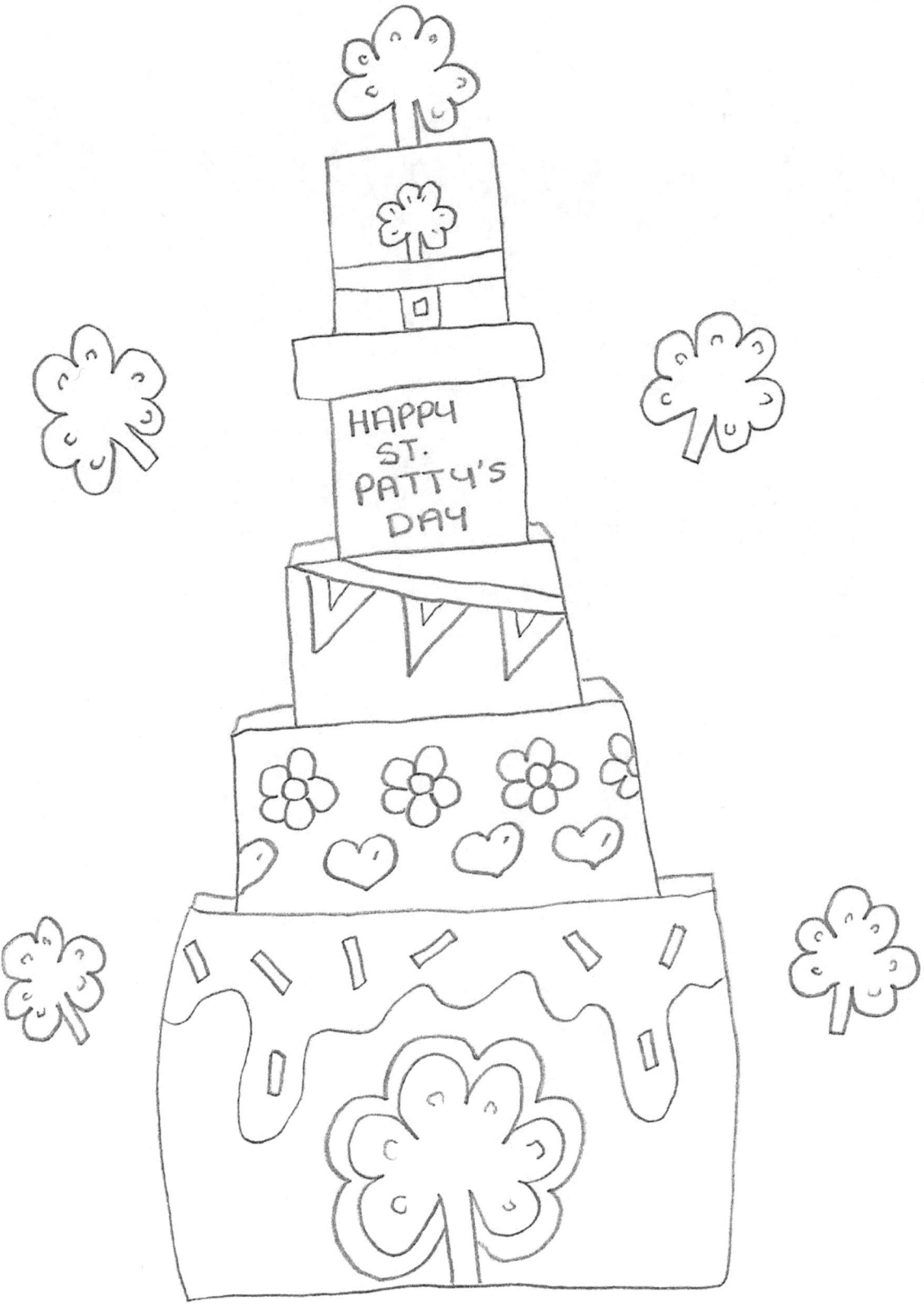

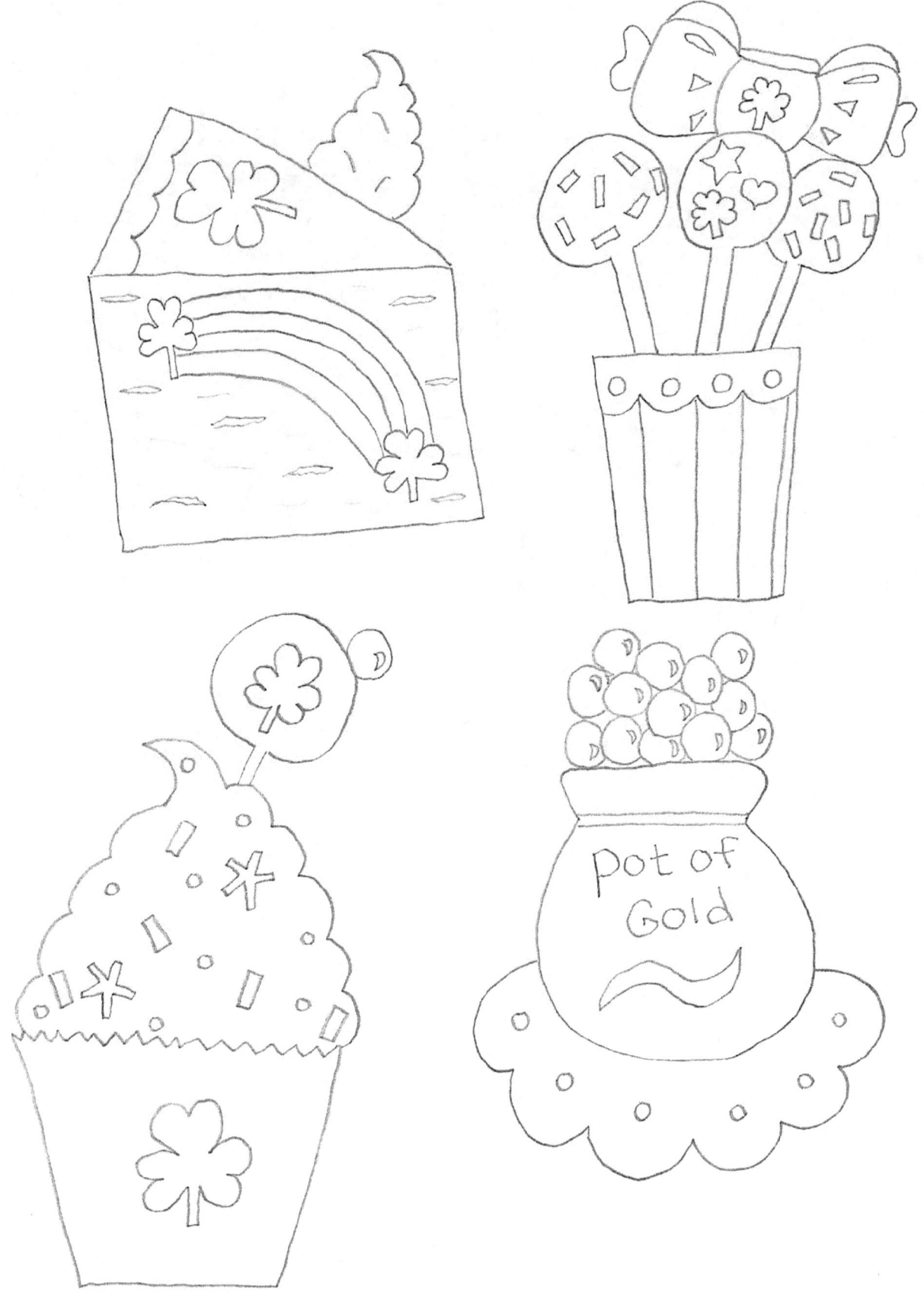

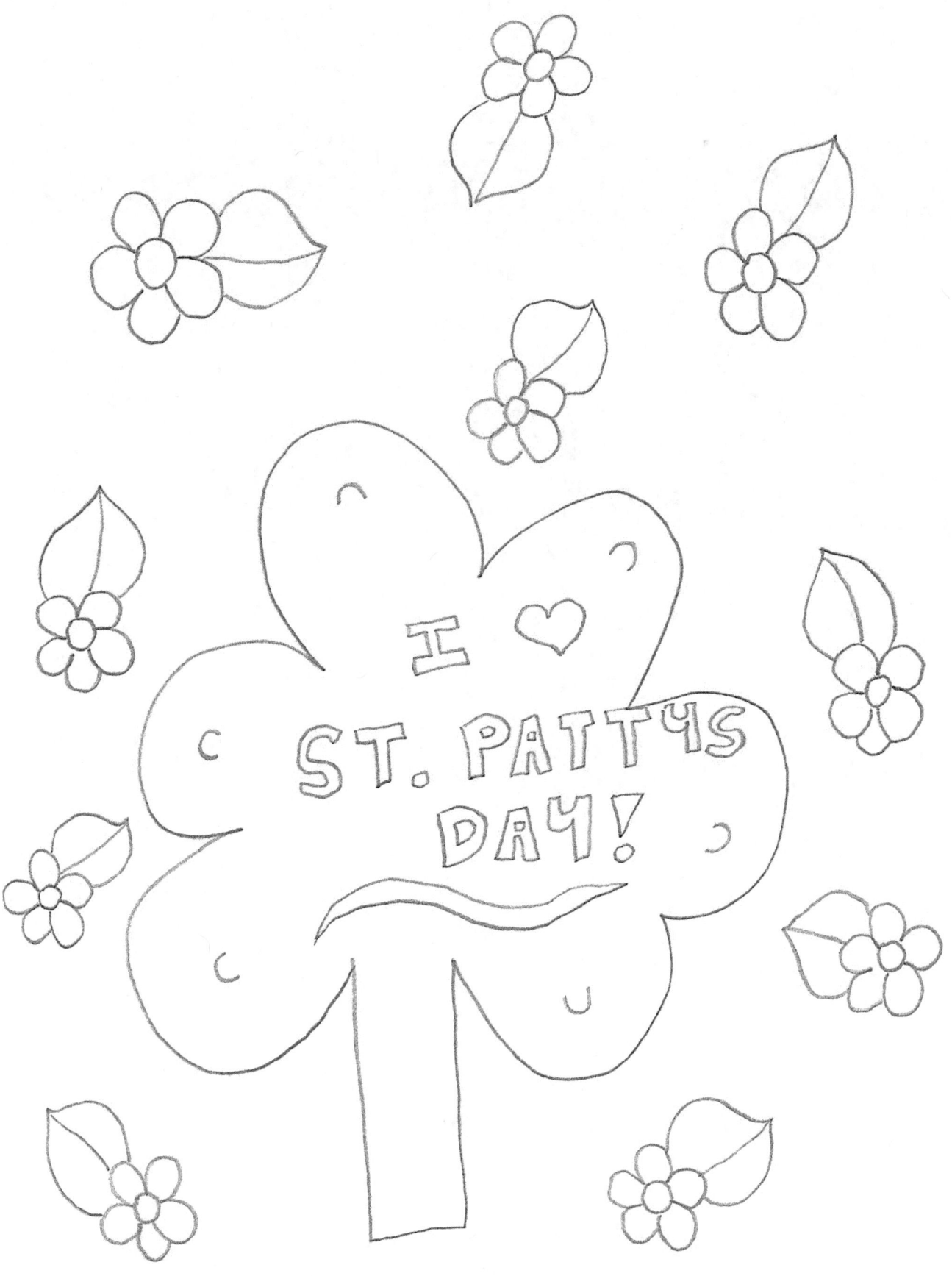

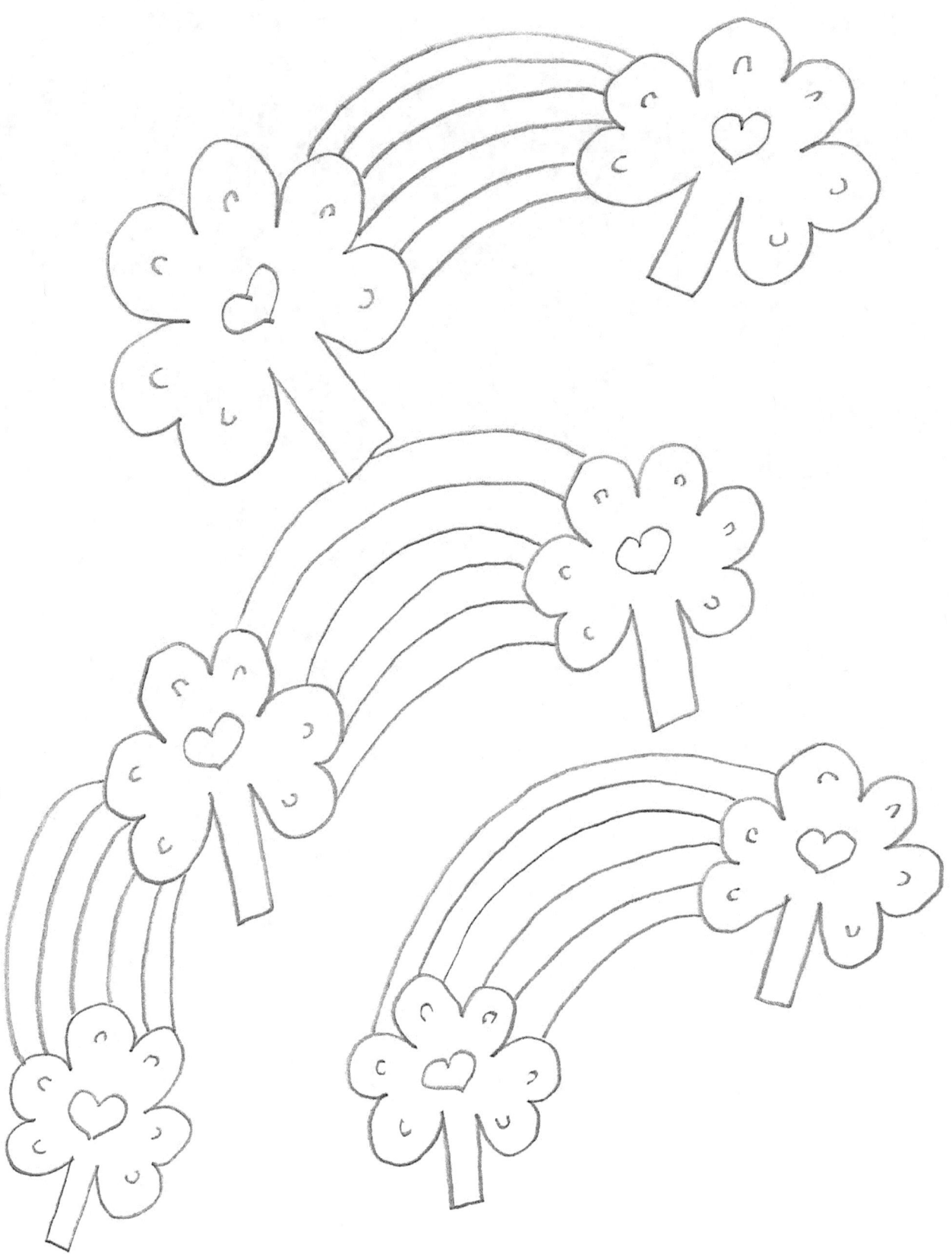

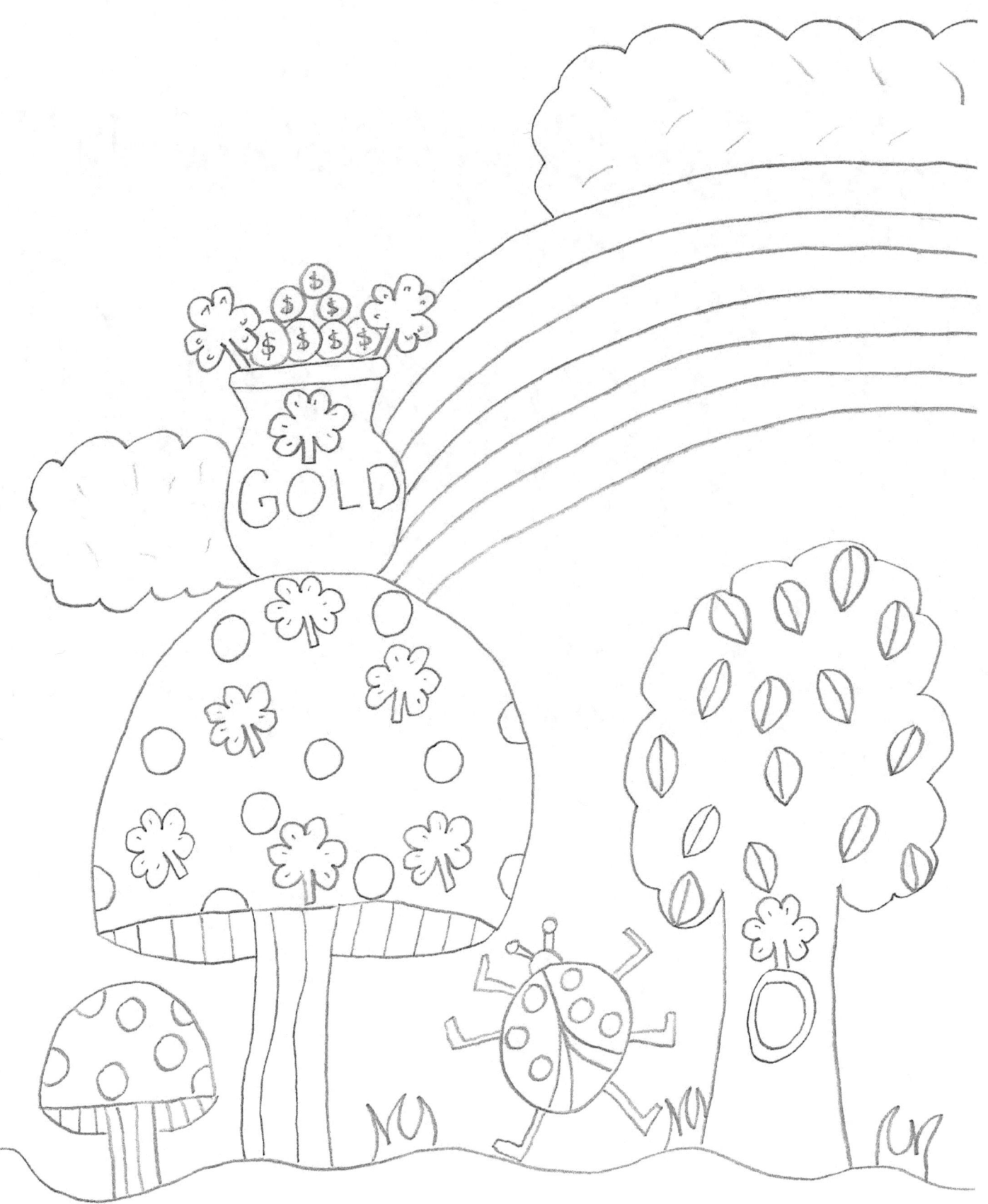

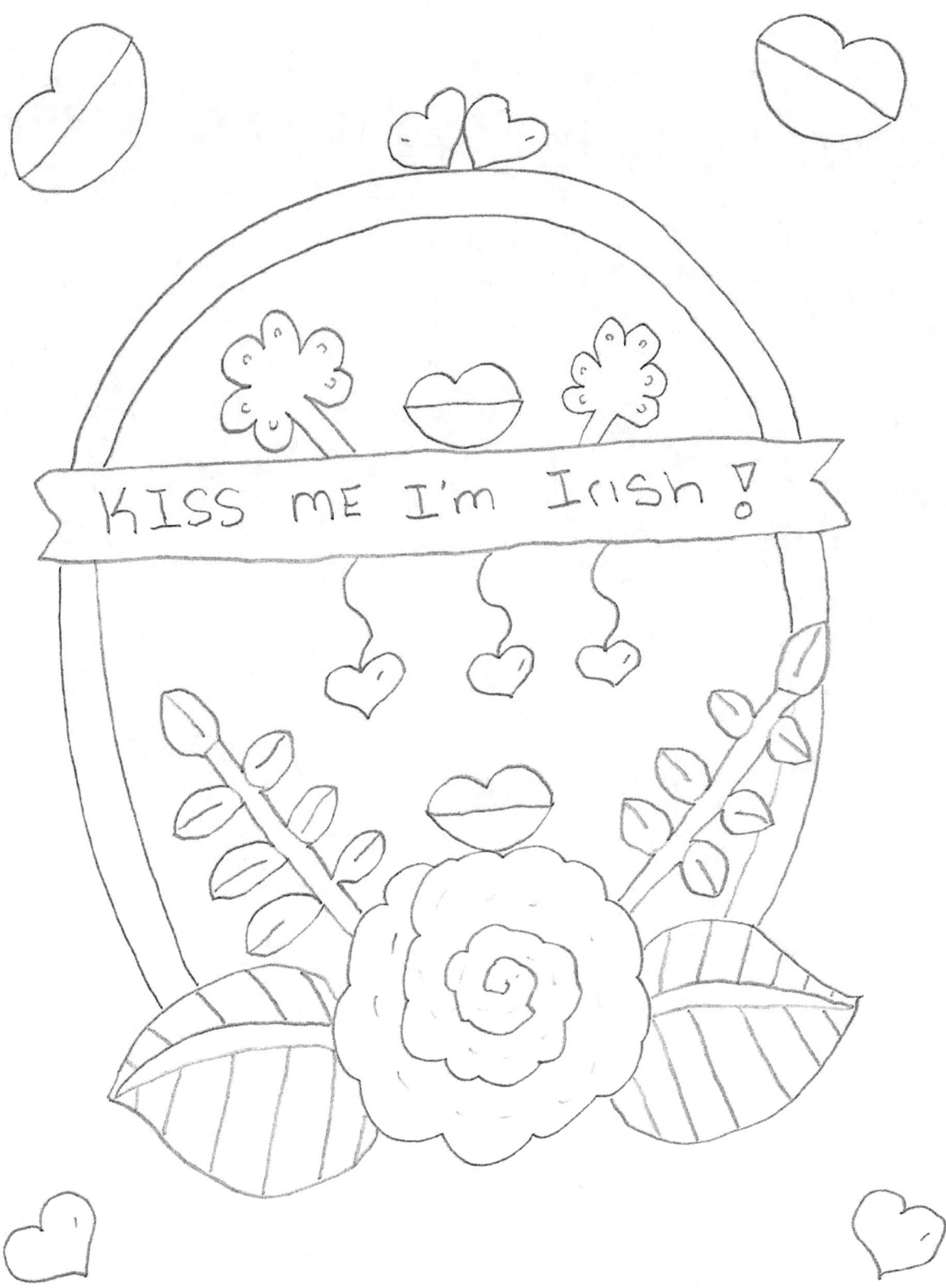

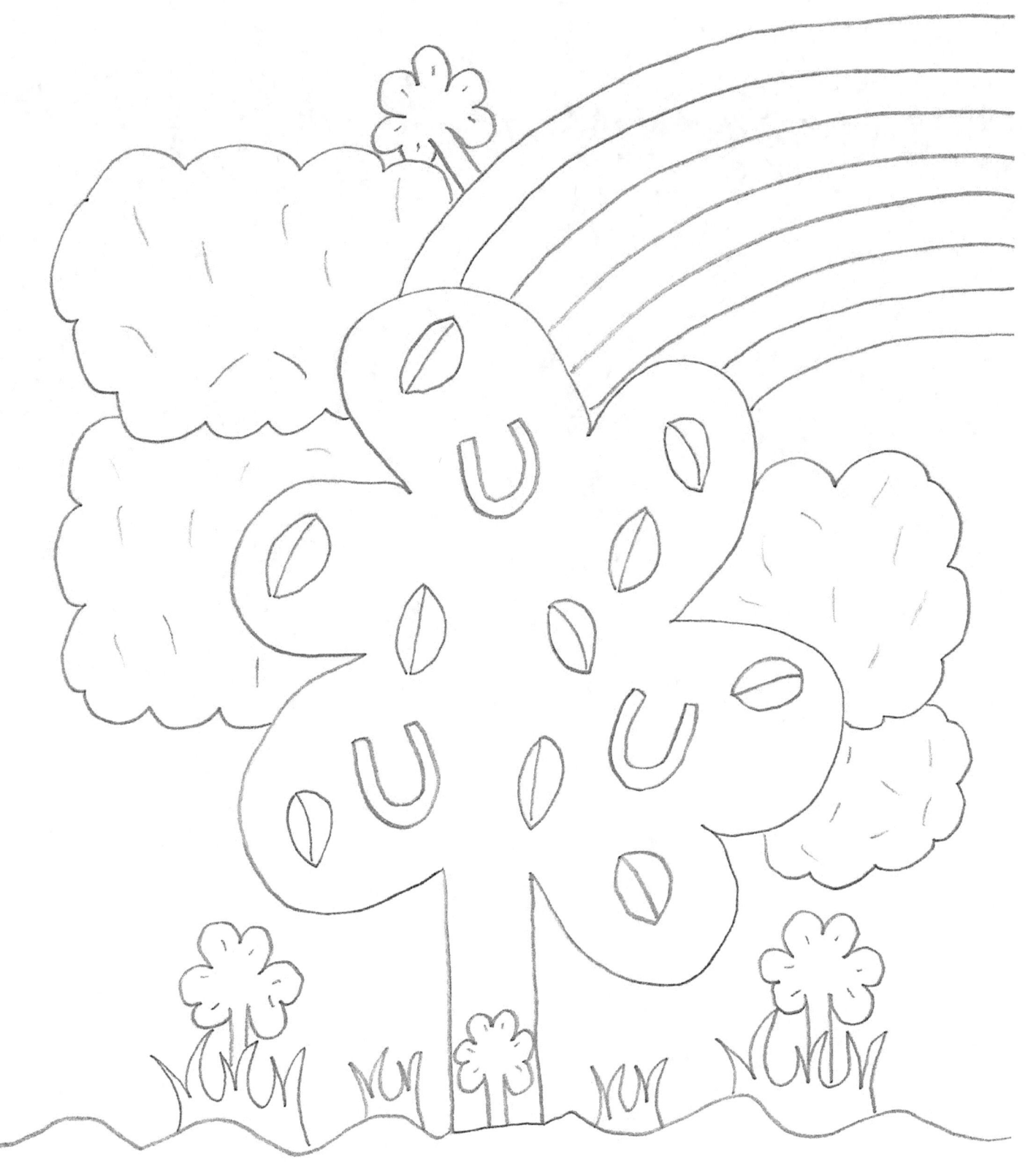

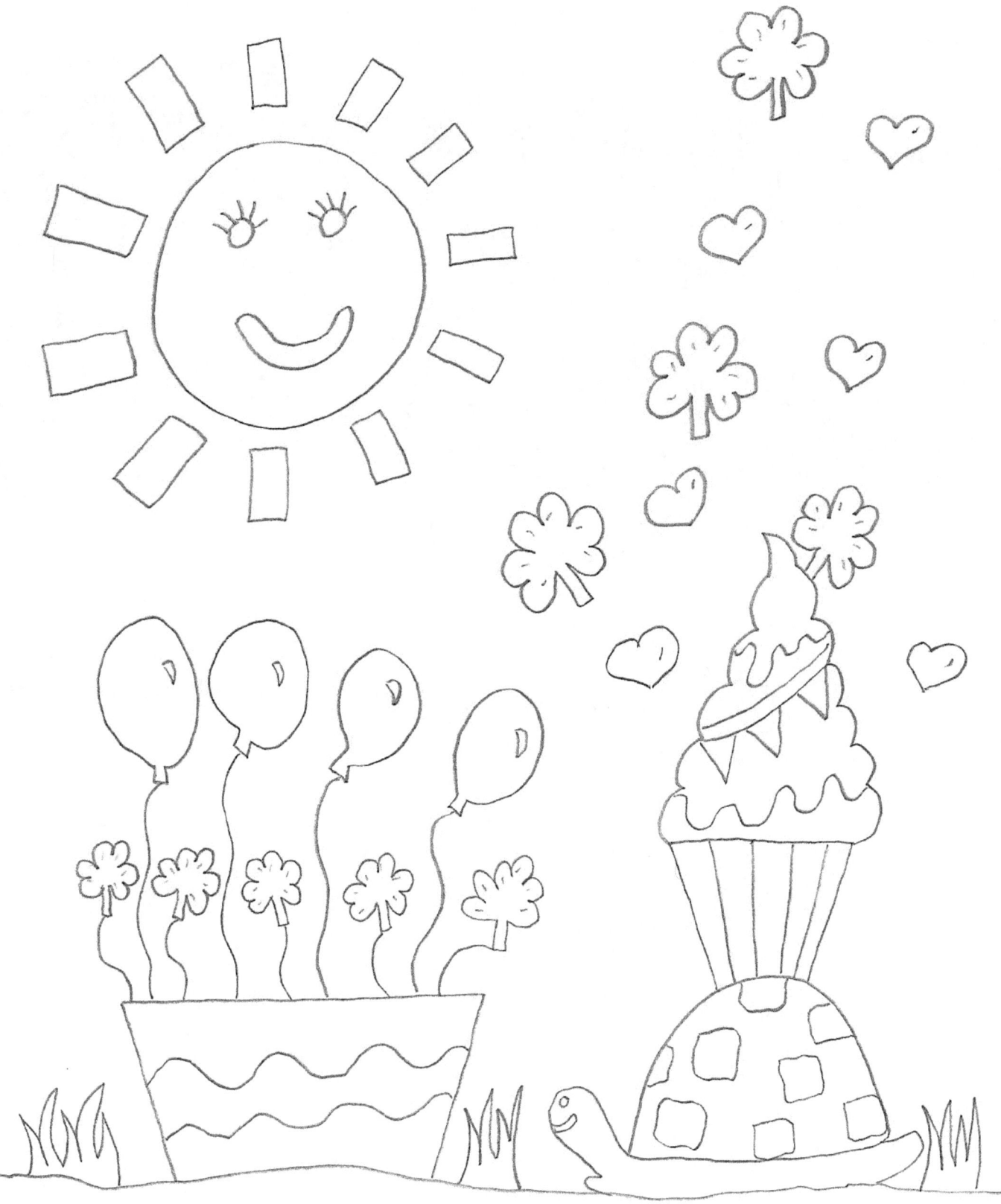

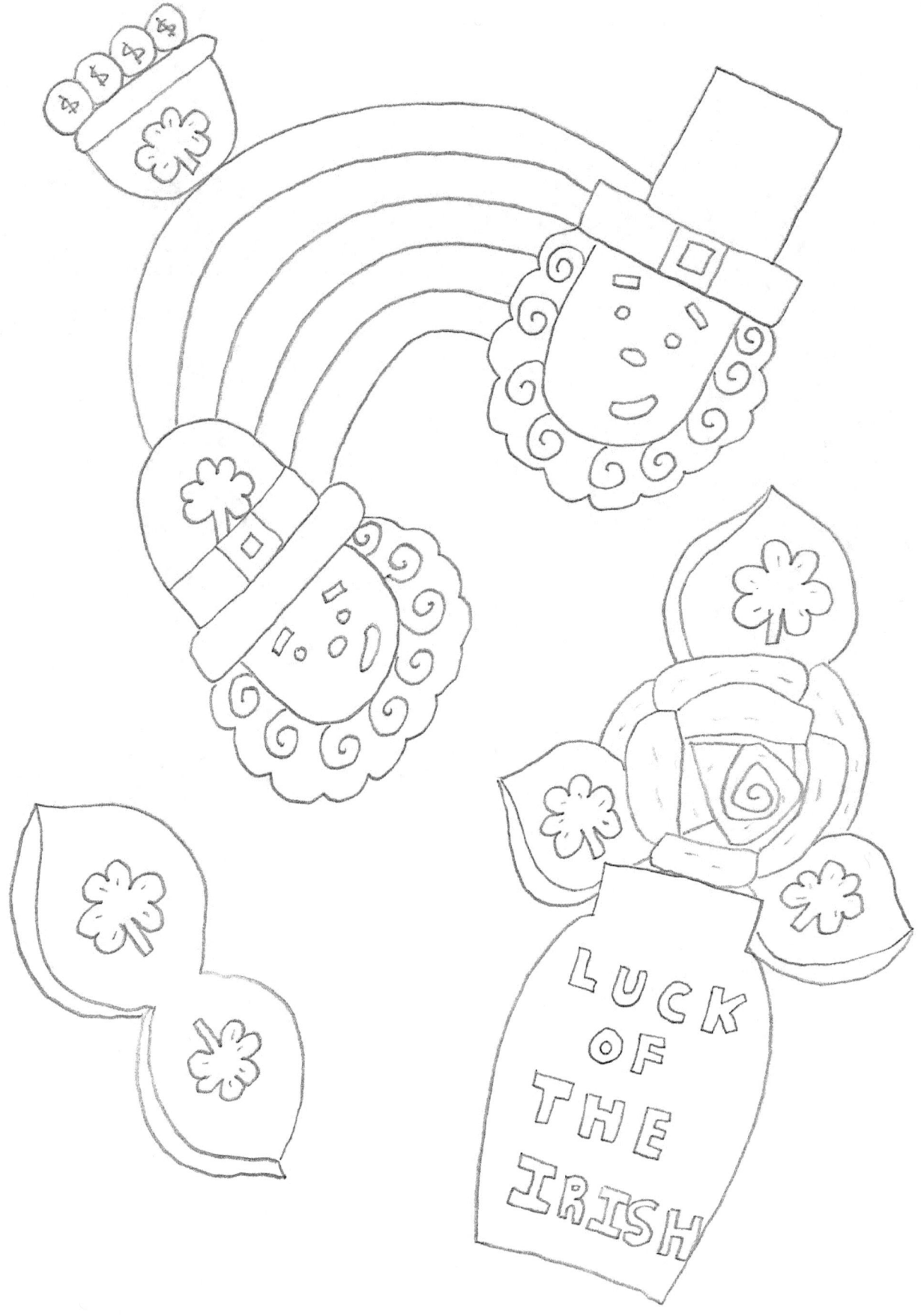

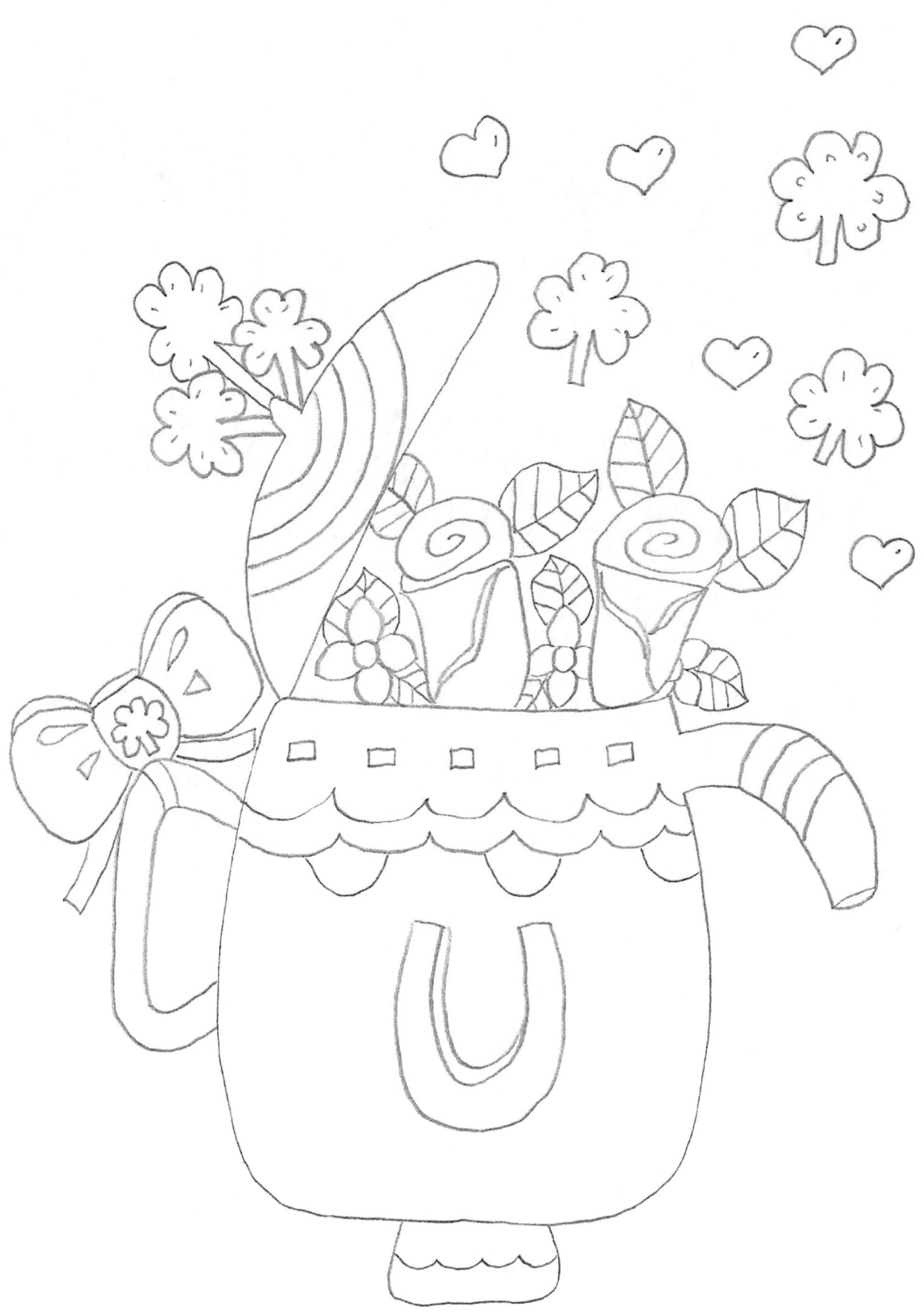

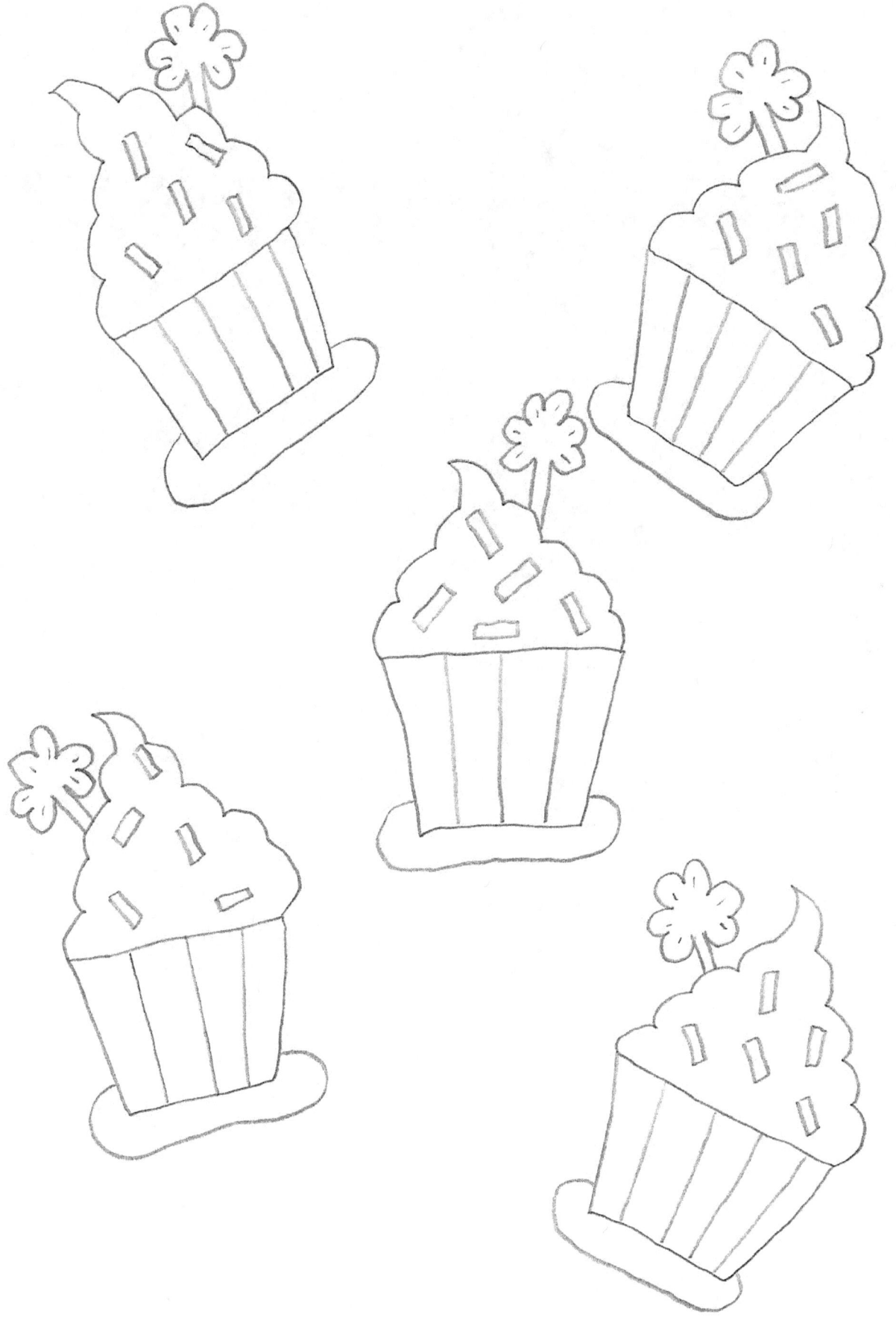

HAPPY
ST.
PATTY'S
DAY!

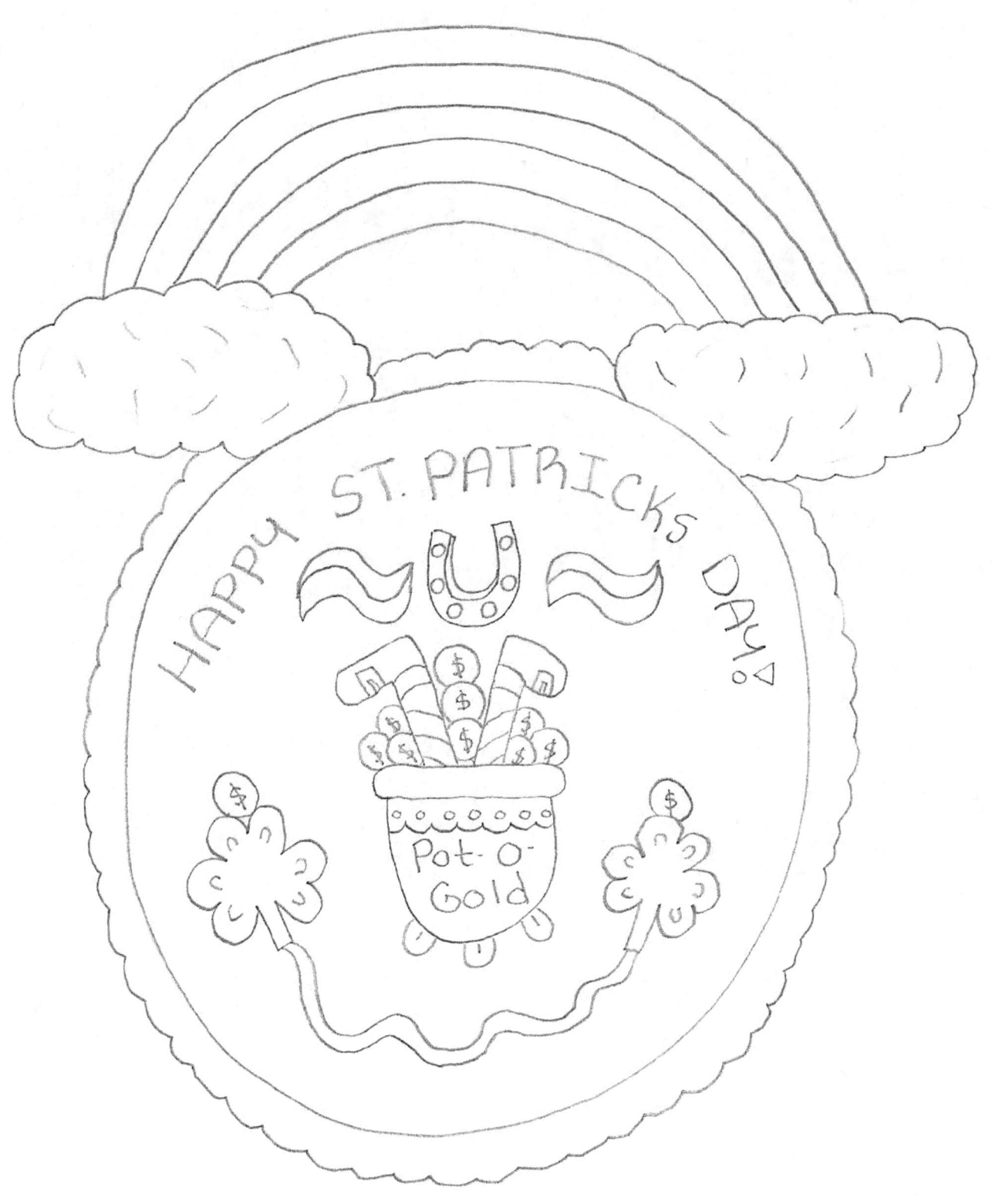

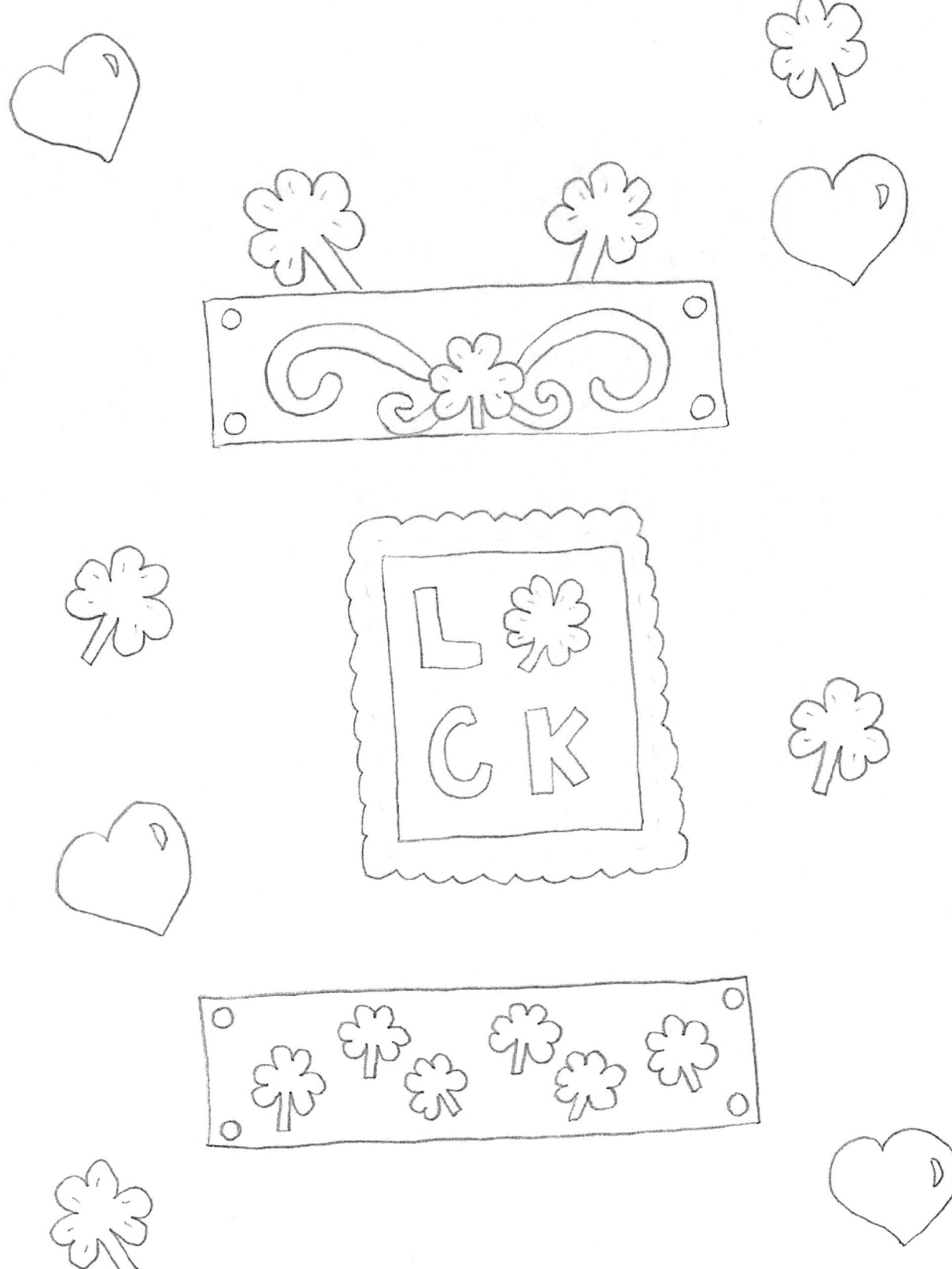

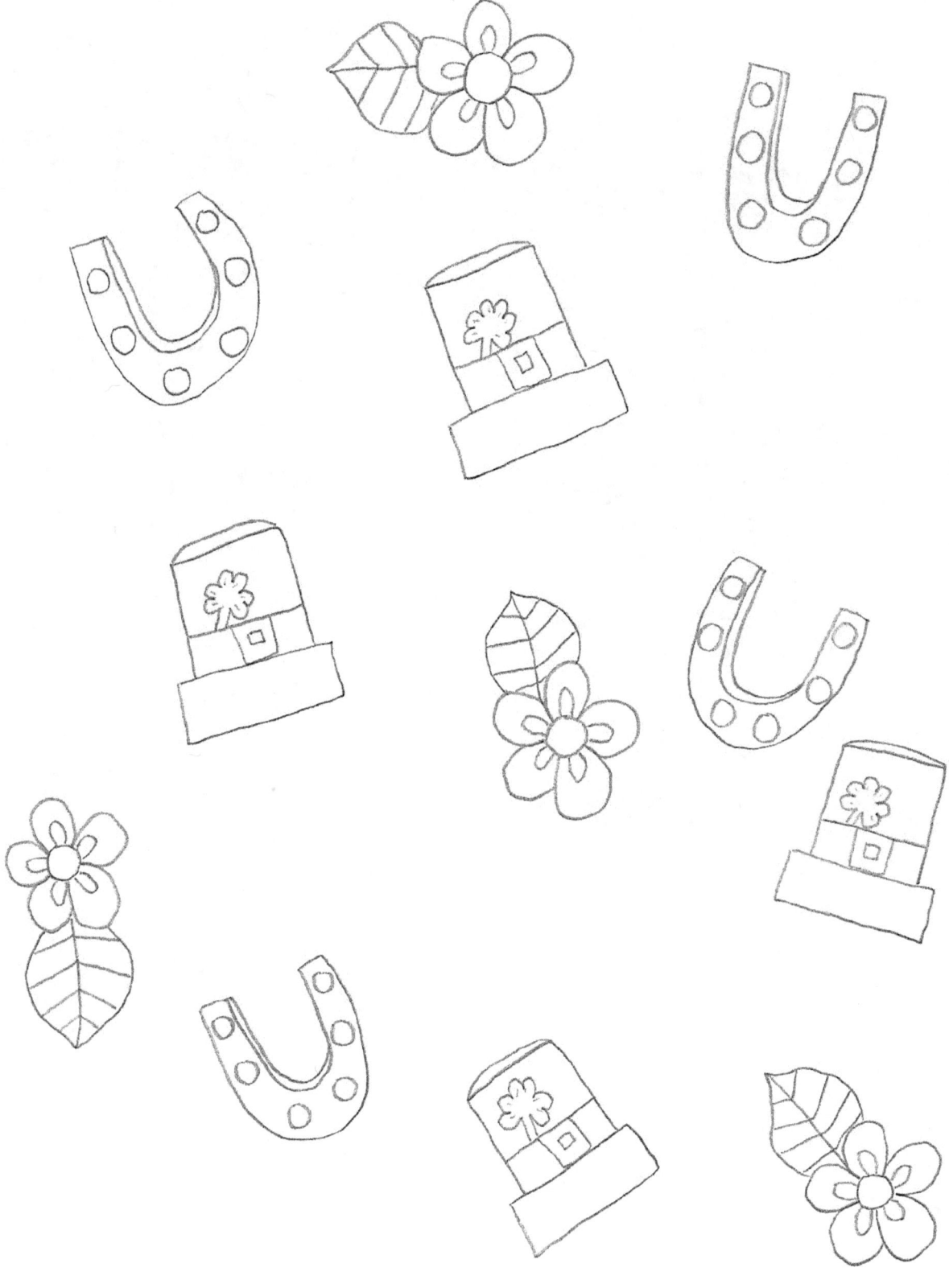

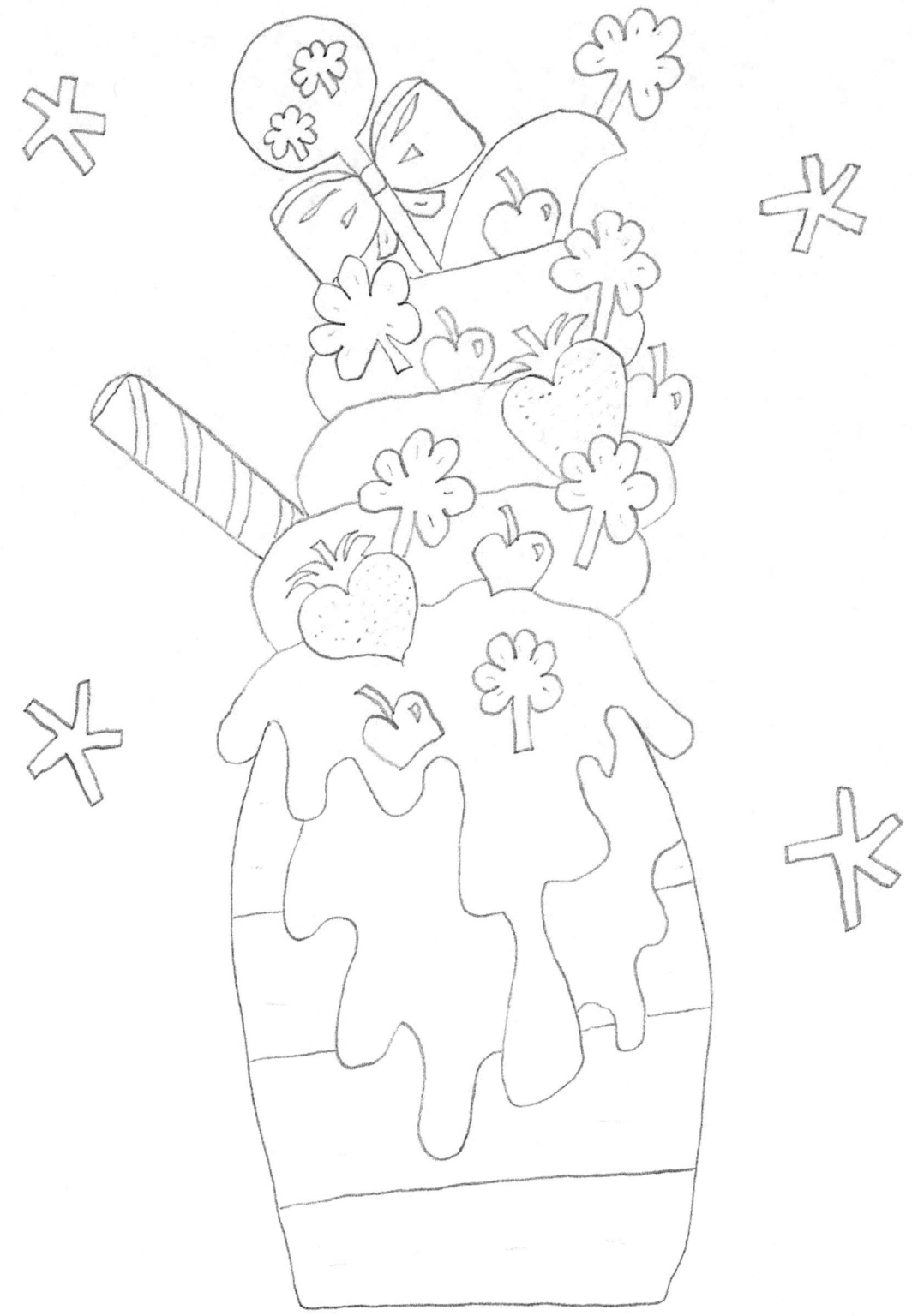

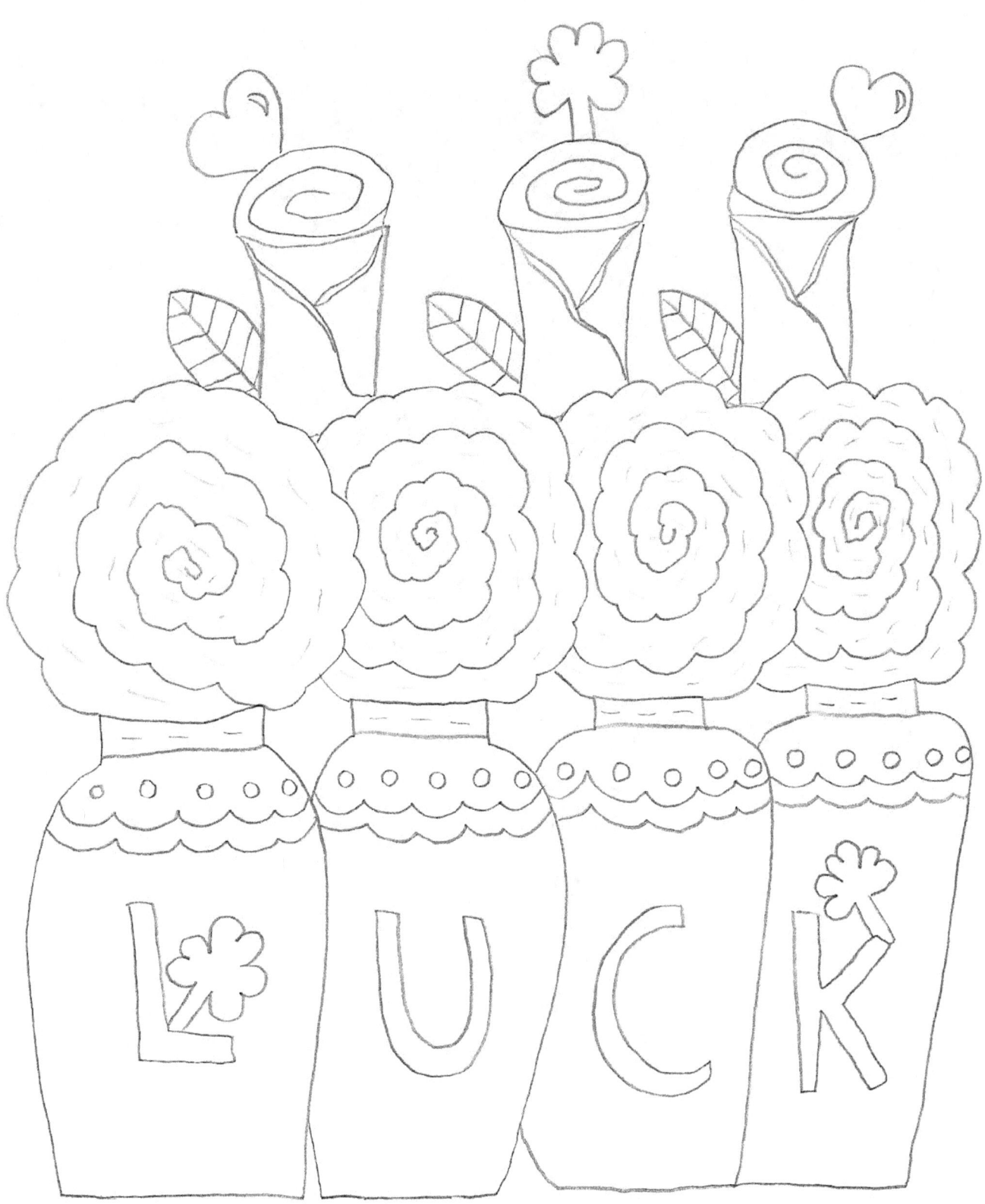

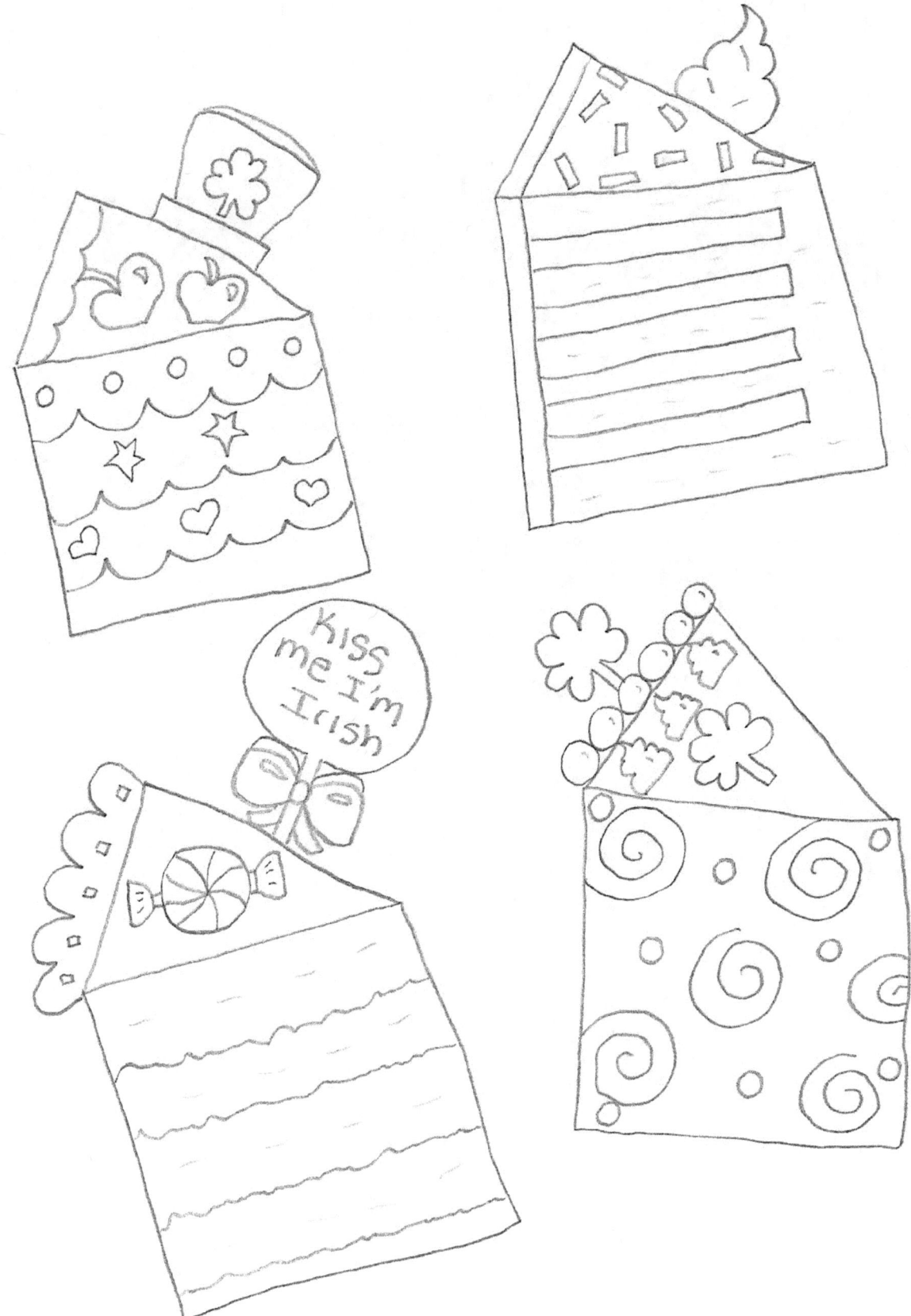

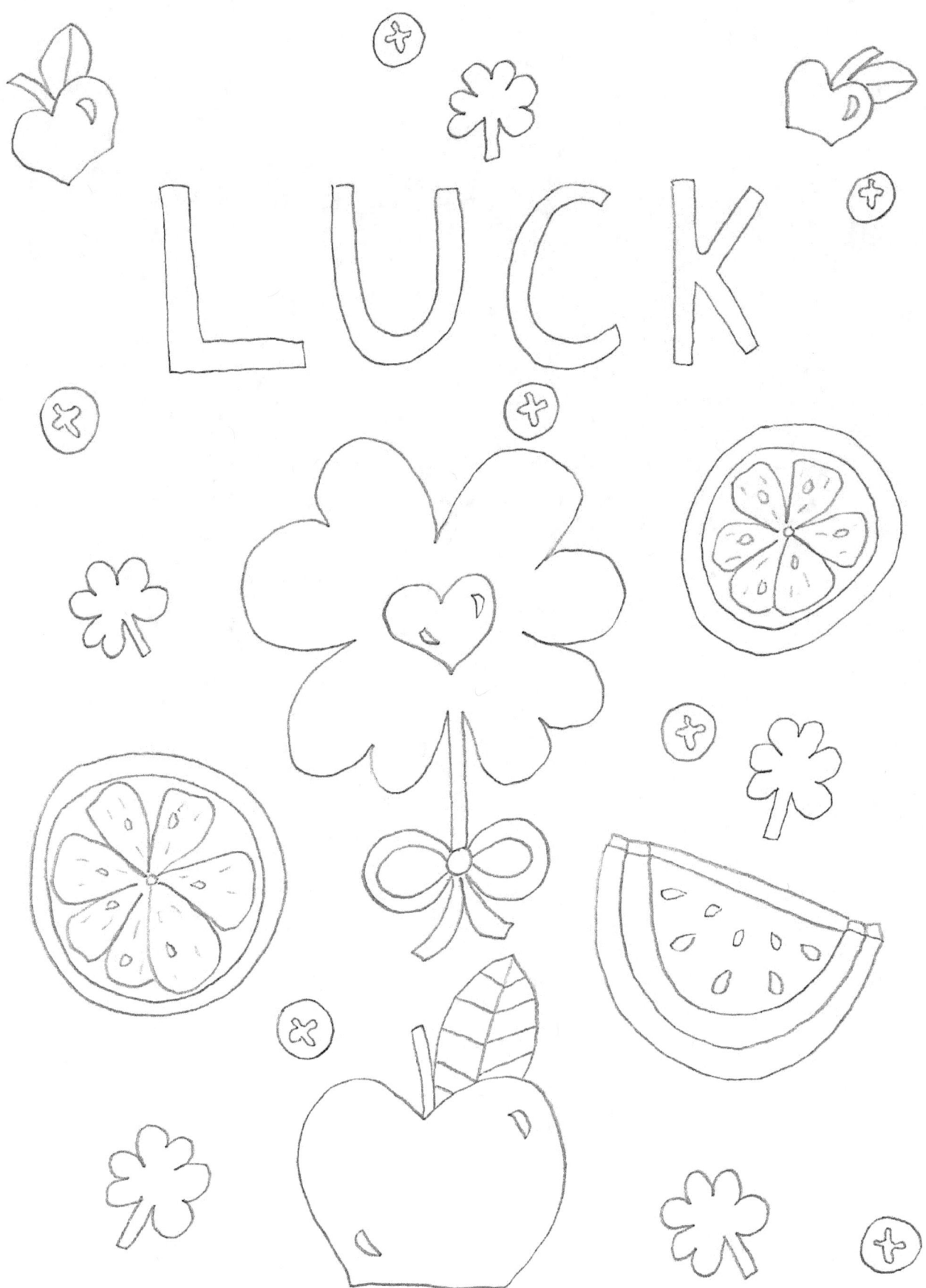

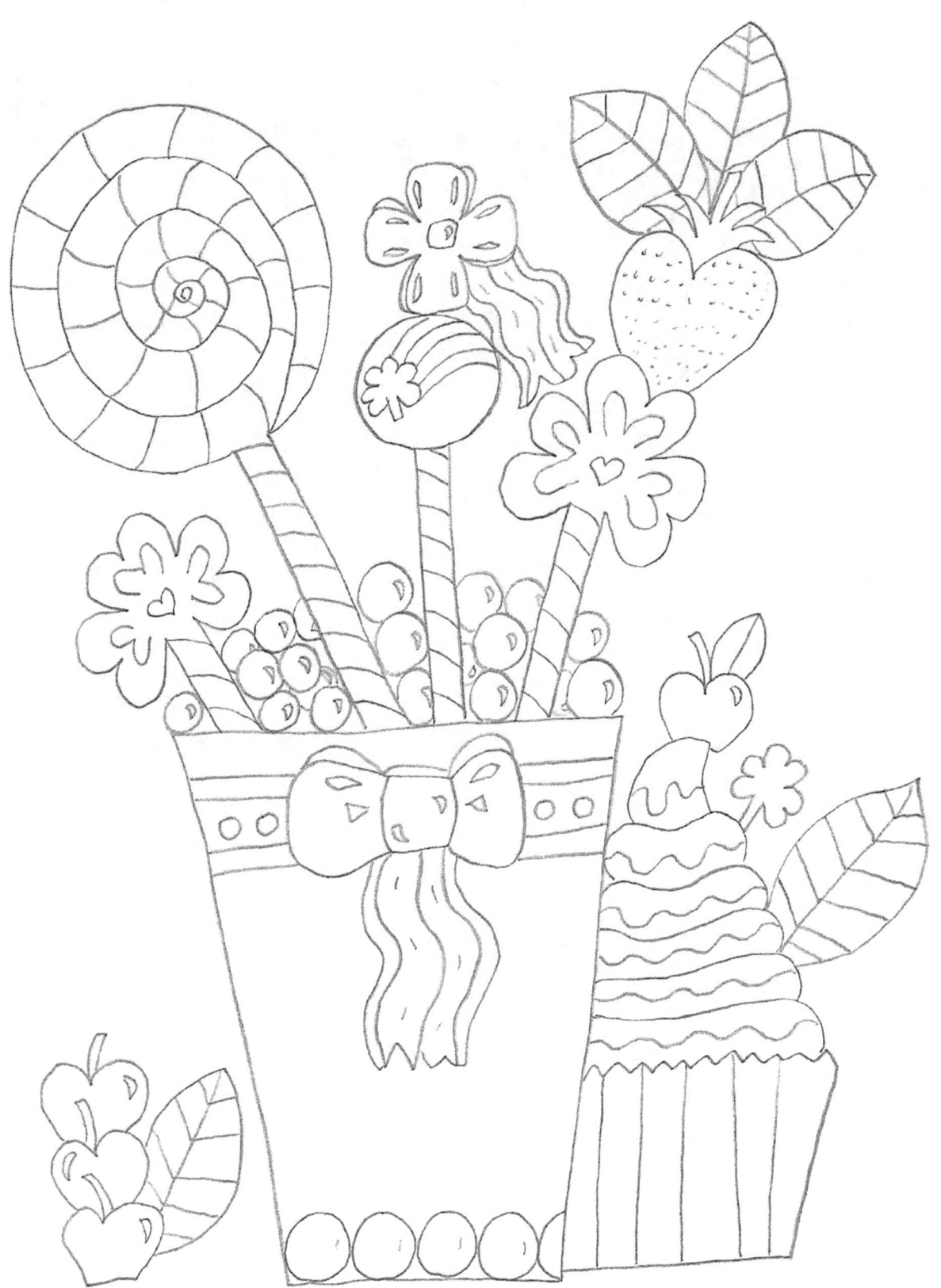

THANK YOU FOR PURCHASING A HAPPY ST. PATTY'S DAY KID'S COLORING BOOK. YOU CAN CHECK OUT MY OTHER COLORING BOOKS LISTED BELOW WHICH CAN BE PURCHASED AT AMAZON.COM:

VINTAGE PARIS BAKE SHOP (Adult)

VINTAGE WINE GARDEN (Adult)

ICE CREAM MADNESS (Adult)

ICE CREAM MADNESS VOLUME 2 (Adult)

TEA & COFFEE TROPICAL TREASURES (Adult)

TEA & COFFEE OCEAN TREASURES (Adult)

TEA & COFFEE TREASURES (Adult)

BOTANICAL FLOWERS & MANDALAS (Adult)

MAJESTIC FALL (Adult)

A VERY RETRO CHRISTMAS (Adult)

MAGICAL DESSERTS (Kids)

MAGICAL DESSERTS VOLUME 2 (Kids)

MAGICAL DESSERTS VOLUME 3 (Kids)

FASHION DOLLS (Adult)

FAIRIES IN THE FLOWER GARDEN (Adult)

MERMAID'S WONDERLAND SEA OF ENCHANTMENT (Adult)

CHRISTMAS DESSERTS

VALENTINE'S DAYDREAMS COLORING BOOK (Adult)

VALENTINE'S DAY DELIGHTS (Adult)

VALENTINE'S FLOWERS & DESSERTS (Adult)

VALENTINE'S DAY DESSERTS (Adult)

VALENTINE'S DAY ANIMALS & Sweets (Kids)

VALENTINE DAY'S FLOWERS (Adult)

A VERY RUSTIC VALENTINE'S DAY (Adult)

ELEGANT FLOWERS (Adult)

ST. PATRICK'S DAY BLESSINGS (Adult)

IF YOU ENJOYED YOUR COLORING EXPERIENCE, PLEASE TELL OTHERS ABOUT IT BY WRITING A REVIEW ON AMAZON.COM UNDER THE BOOK YOU COLORED.